FASCINATING

THE LIFE OF LEONARD NIMOY

BY RICHARD MICHELSON

ILLUSTRATED BY EDEL RODRIGUEZ

ALFRED A. KNOPF   NEW YORK

For Leonard (in memoriam) and Susan, with gratitude.

Thank you for welcoming me into your lives.

"I have been, and always shall be, your friend."

—R.M.

For Gabrielle and Sofia

—E.R.

THIS IS A BORZOI BOOK PUBLISHED BY ALFRED A. KNOPF

Text copyright © 2016 by Richard Michelson
Jacket art and interior illustrations copyright © 2016 by Edel Rodriguez
The character Mr. Spock is copyrighted by CBS Studios Inc., 1966.

Visit us on the Web! randomhousekids.com

Educators and librarians, for a variety of teaching tools, visit us at RHTeachersLibrarians.com

Library of Congress Cataloging-in-Publication Data
Names: Michelson, Richard, author. | Rodriguez, Edel, illustrator.
Title: Fascinating : the life of Leonard Nimoy / by Richard Michelson ; illustrated by Edel Rodriguez.
Description: First edition. | New York : Alfred A. Knopf, 2016
Identifiers: LCCN 2015029967 | ISBN 978-1-101-93330-5 (trade) | ISBN 978-1-101-93331-2 (lib. bdg.)
ISBN 978-1-101-93332-9 (ebook)
Subjects: LCSH: Nimoy, Leonard—Juvenile literature. | Actors—United States—Biography—
Juvenile literature.
Classification: LCC PN2287.N55 M53 2016 | DDC 791.4302/8092—dc23

The text of this book is set in 11-point ITC Avant Garde Gothic.

MANUFACTURED IN CHINA
September 2016
10 9 8 7 6 5 4 3 2 1

First Edition

Lenny took a deep breath and looked out at the playhouse stage. Just that morning, he had been shooting baskets in the gym at the Elizabeth Peabody settlement house. He hadn't even known the building had a theater.

But Mr. Chalfin, the new social director, had heard Lenny chanting the *Shema* prayer with his father at Temple Beth Israel, and he needed someone to sing "God Bless America" to open tonight's talent show.

Lenny peered out at the audience from behind the curtain. Was every person in Boston's West End here? He could see Stanley and George, his best friends since kindergarten. Now it was 1939, and they were in the third grade. And there was his brother, Mel, still wearing his high school science-lab apron.

In the front row sat two empty chairs. One had a handwritten sign that said RESERVED FOR MAX NIMOY. The other said AND DORA. Finally, Lenny saw his mother hurrying down the aisle with a big grin on her face. His father, following, was still wearing his barber's smock. He must have come straight from his shop, where he'd been cutting hair since immigrating to Boston from Russia sixteen years ago.

When they arrived in this country, Max's and Dora's passports were stamped "alien," and that was how they still felt. But they trusted the settlement house, which taught immigrant families to "be American." There were classes in how to boil hot dogs, and how to brush your teeth with a toothbrush instead of a rag. "There is so much to know, it makes me dizzy," Max would moan.

The houselights went down, and the footlights went up. "Reach for the stars," Mr. Chalfin said as Lenny stepped onto the stage.

Walking home with his family, Lenny couldn't stop whistling. "Such clapping
I never heard before," his mother said, beaming.

The neighbors leaned out their windows to offer congratulations. "Bravo,"
Mr. Basso boomed. "May luck be your friend forever, lad," Mrs. Kernan sang out. Most
of the neighbors were Italian or Irish. Lenny could find his way home with his eyes closed,
just by following the smells that wafted from each tenement kitchen. Garlic meant they
were passing the Grecos' apartment and were almost at 87 Chambers Street, where
he shared four small rooms with Mel, his parents, and his bubbe and zayde.

Most all the kids in the building got along, but every Sunday Lenny felt left out when his friends went to church. Still, he felt special when his father took him to shul. On Rosh Hashanah, the Jewish New Year, Lenny watched the men in front start swaying and singing a special prayer.

"We're supposed to cover our eyes during the priestly blessing," Max whispered. "So don't look. No cheating."

Lenny peeked. He was fascinated by what he saw. The men pulled their prayer shawls over their heads, but their chants only got louder. As they blessed the congregation, they raised both arms in the air and held out their hands as if they were shooting a two-handed jump shot. What were they doing with their fingers? Fascinating.

He couldn't ask, or his father would know he'd disobeyed.

That night in his room, Lenny practiced what he'd witnessed. He taped together his index finger and middle finger. Then his pinkie and ring finger.

By the time of his bar mitzvah, Lenny could make the gesture easily with either hand. His fingers looked like the letter *shin,* which, he'd learned in Hebrew school, was the first letter of the word *shalom,* or "peace," and *Shaddai,* one of the names for God.

After school, Lenny peddled newspapers on Beacon Hill. He learned everything important that was going on in the world when he shouted out the day's headlines. Plus, he made a penny and a half for every *Record* he sold. Some evenings he also stacked chairs at the band shell.

Once he stayed too late, and Max and Dora came looking for him. "It isn't safe to be out after dark!" his father yelled. He grabbed the two dollars Lenny had been paid, ripped each bill in half, and threw them to the ground. But Lenny saw his mother pick up the torn bills before she started home. Money was hard to come by, and a little Scotch tape could fix anything.

At home, Bubbe made him feel better. She sang him a Yiddish song about a boy who wanted to turn into a bird and explore the planet.

Zayde added, "Go, do, discover! Our world is a fascinating place. Your parents worry because they love you, but sometimes too much love can clip your wings."

Lenny was saving every penny he made. The family had gotten a Kodak bellows camera, and he needed film to take some pictures. He tried to capture all the wisdom and wit in Zayde's face. *Click.*

For the first time he noticed the sad lines around Bubbe's eyes. *Click.*

Next he studied his mother and father through the viewfinder. He had never looked at them so closely. He could always tell what his mother was thinking. *Click.*

But his father mostly hid his emotions. *Click.*

Lenny knew you needed a dark room without any windows to develop pictures, so he closed the door to the family bathroom and turned out the light. Slowly he watched each image emerge. "Fascinating!" It was magic. He was exposing his family's souls.

When Lenny was seventeen, he heard that the settlement house theater was putting on a performance of *Awake and Sing!* by the playwright Clifford Odets. It was about three generations of a poor Jewish family who lived together in one small apartment. The director needed someone to play the part of the son, who yearned for a better life and a society where everyone was treated fairly. Lenny read the play. Could the author have known the Nimoys? How did Mr. Odets understand what Lenny was thinking—thoughts he hadn't shared with *anyone*?

HOLLYWOOD

Lenny loved performing. He tried out for every play he could. Each character was different, and he always tried to figure out their hopes and dreams, and their secrets, too. He was in a play at a local temple when Father John Bonn came backstage. "What are you doing this summer?" he asked.

"I have nothing planned," Lenny answered.

"Well, you do now, son," the priest said. He invited Lenny to attend the Boston College summer theater program on scholarship.

By August, Lenny knew he wanted to be a professional actor. His parents had traveled across the ocean in pursuit of a better life. Now he would travel across the country to Hollywood to follow his dreams.

But train travel was expensive. Where would he get the money?

Ace Vacuum Cleaners was hiring door-to-door salesmen. "You offer a cheap Electrolux for ten dollars," the boss told him. "But once you get past the front door, you have to talk the housewife into spending one hundred dollars for a fancy machine."

The first few women slammed the door in his face. The next two let Lenny demonstrate the product, but they didn't buy anything. Maybe he was too quiet and honest for this job. Then he had an idea. Lenny pretended he was on stage, playing the part of a confident, and slightly shady, salesman. Soon he had a pocket full of money.

In September 1949, he was standing at South Station, wearing a blue double-breasted suit from Filene's Basement and holding a train ticket to California. His mother gave him a hug goodbye. There were tears in her eyes. "May you live till one hundred and twenty, and have a long and healthy life like Moses."

"Learn to play the accordion," his father called out as he stepped onto the *20th Century Limited*. "Actors starve, but at least musicians can eke out a living."

Hollywood was hot. And everyone dressed casually. Leonard felt like an outsider as he looked for the Pasadena Playhouse, where he would study acting. He was sweating in his wool suit, but he had no time to change his clothes. He was too eager to change his life.

Leonard worked as a movie theater usher, then a soda jerk. Next he drove a taxi so that he could be available for auditions during the day.

One night, he picked up a man with a Boston accent. Leonard felt homesick. Maybe his father was right. He should forget his dreams and head home. But his passenger advised, "Never give up as long as you can make a difference in people's lives. Lots of competition in your business, just like in mine. But an actor is like a politician. There is always room at the top for one more good one." He handed Leonard his business card: CONGRESSMAN JOHN F. KENNEDY.

Leonard took the future president's advice. He worked hard, learned his lines, showed up on time, and studied his craft. When he turned twenty, he got a small part in a movie called *Queen for a Day.* Next he played a Martian invader in *Zombies of the Stratosphere,* and finally he got his first starring role as "Kid" Monk Baroni. He was only paid $350, but his name was on a Boston West End movie theater marquee. He was on his way!

For the next thirteen years, he continued to act, mostly in television series. He also opened his own studio to help teach younger performers. He got married and had two children, Julie and Adam.

Then one day in 1965, he got a call from Gene Roddenberry, a producer who was writing a new science-fiction television show called *Star Trek*. He wanted Leonard to play the part of an alien science officer named Spock. He explained that Spock worked with earthlings on a starship named the *Enterprise,* which would take the crew to explore many new worlds. But Spock would always feel like an outsider because his father was from a planet called Vulcan, where everyone made decisions based on logic instead of emotion.

Leonard wasn't sure he wanted the part. He would have to wear pointy ears and a silly haircut. What if the audience made fun of him and his career was ruined? He tried to think about his decision logically. Then he remembered looking at his own father through the camera lens and seeing all the hidden emotion in his face. And he remembered how Zayde always encouraged him to take chances. And he remembered Mr. Chalfin from back home, who told him to reach for the stars.

"My folks came to the United States as immigrants. They were called aliens, and they became citizens," he told Mr. Roddenberry. "I was born in Boston, as a citizen, then I came to Hollywood as an outsider, and now it is time for me to become an alien. I *am* Spock."

Leonard poured all of his experience into the role. And people everywhere identified with Spock's attempts to fit in, even though he was different. They cheered as he stood up to bullies, argued for justice, and tried to convince everyone that it made sense to live peacefully.

Back home in Boston, boys started coming into Max Nimoy's barbershop asking for a "Spock haircut." Max even taped a picture of his son, the science officer, to the mirror. He was proud that Leonard was making a good living. But he still didn't understand what all the fuss was about.

In *Star Trek*'s second season, the *Enterprise* visited the planet Vulcan. It was the first time viewers would see the world Spock came from. The script told Spock to shake hands with the Vulcan queen. But Leonard wanted to have a special greeting. "Asians bow when they meet," he told the director, "and military men salute."

"And how do Vulcans greet each other?" he was asked.

Leonard thought for a while, and then he remembered his time in the temple when he was eight years old. He held up his hand in the ancient Hebraic gesture. And he blessed the actors he worked with, and he blessed the audience, and he blessed everyone all over the universe.

"Live long and prosper."

LEONARD NIMOY received three Emmy nominations for his portrayal of Spock on *Star Trek.* He received an additional nomination for playing Golda Meir's husband in *A Woman Called Golda.* And he was lauded for his portrayal of the Holocaust survivor Mel Mermelstein in *Never Forget.* In 2014, he was presented with an Emmy Award for Lifetime Achievement from the National Academy of Television Arts and Sciences.

Star Trek lasted only three seasons but has developed into one of the most well-regarded programs in television history, with a large and dedicated fan base, who call themselves Trekkies or Trekkers. There are now *Star Trek* games, novels, toys, exhibits, comics, and conventions. *Star Trek* has had a great influence on both popular and scientific culture. Many inventions, such as the cell phone, were inspired by props or ideas explored on the program. And some of our best science-fiction authors wrote for the show,

including Theodore Sturgeon, who penned the phrase "Live long and prosper" in the episode "Amok Time." There have been six movies based on the original series, two of which Leonard directed. (Four additional movies were based on *Star Trek: The Next Generation,* and more recent films, starring Zachary Quinto as the younger Spock, explore the time period prior to the original series.) Leonard also directed other popular movies, such as *Three Men and a Baby,* which was the biggest box-office hit of 1987.

Over the years, Leonard continued to explore many artistic worlds that he first learned to love as a child back in Boston. He recorded five albums of music and wrote seven books of poetry. He wrote two biographies, *I Am Not Spock* and *I Am Spock.* He both wrote and performed in *Vincent,* his critically acclaimed play about the artist Vincent van Gogh. Among other roles, he starred in *Equus* on Broadway and toured the country as Tevye in *Fiddler on the Roof,* King

Arthur in *Camelot,* and Sherlock Holmes in a Royal Shakespeare Company production.

He continued taking pictures and, in 1971, he enrolled at UCLA to further his photography studies. His book *Shekhina* was published in 2002. *Shekhina* is the feminine aspect of God, also known as the divine presence on earth, and Leonard finally learned the reason his father told him to look away during the priestly blessing so many years ago. A Jewish mystical tradition teaches that when the *Shekhina* is invoked to bless the congregation—"May God's face shine on you"—the beauty and truth of Her light is so overwhelming that if you gaze at it directly, you might be blinded. Leonard published three additional volumes of his photography, *The Full Body Project, Secret Selves,* and a limited-edition portfolio called *Eye Contact.* His work has been exhibited in, and collected by, major museums throughout the country.

With his wife, Susan Bay Nimoy, Leonard started a private foundation to help young visual artists, and throughout his lifetime he continued to speak for political causes that helped bring peace and social justice to all people.

He became one of the world's most recognized, beloved, and honored personalities.

But he never did learn to play the accordion.

AUTHOR'S NOTE

SILVIA MAUTNER PHOTOGRAPHY

One of the great privileges of my life is to have enjoyed a professional relationship with Leonard Nimoy, which grew into a deep friendship. He was a fine-art photographer, and I was his gallerist. It was a source of amusement to us both to be regularly mistaken for father and son, but over the years Leonard did indeed become much like a father to me. I was the beneficiary of his advice, spirit, creativity, and generosity. We often traveled together and would reminisce about our childhoods. I had written numerous books about historical figures and Yiddish culture (one of which Leonard recorded), but it never occurred to me to take notes on his life until I saw *Leonard Nimoy's Boston,* Adam Nimoy's inspirational documentary about his father.

I went home and started work on *Fascinating* that evening. Months later, I sent my draft to Leonard. It was Thanksgiving morning 2014, and I heard back immediately in an email. (Leonard was the most prompt and faithful correspondent I have ever had. A quick computer scan tells me we exchanged 3,459 emails over the final ten years of his life, almost one per day.) *It's wonderful and I'm flattered. . . . It is an amazing piece of work and I love that you decided to do it.*

That evening, after finishing the turkey, Leonard wrote again with some corrections—names, dates, and a very few edits. He was looking forward to publication, and the last conversation we had was about this book. It was late February 2015, and he was in the hospital. I told him I expected him to get well and join me on the hoped-for book tour. He laughed and promised he'd be there whenever I called. He passed away soon after. But we do continue to travel together; he remains daily in my thoughts and my heart.

My wife and I consider ourselves blessed to have known Leonard; his loving wife, Susan; his son, Adam; his daughter, Julie; his stepson, Aaron; his brother, Mel; and his extended family. But the gifts he has given to all of us—his acting, his photography, his poetry, his presence—will surely live long and prosper.